INDEX *of* WOMEN

INDEX *of* WOMEN

AMY GERSTLER

PENGUIN POETS

PENGUIN BOOKS

An imprint of Penguin Random House LLC
penguinrandomhouse.com

Pages 85–89 constitute an extension of this copyright page.

Excerpt from "Barbie Chang Got Her Hair Done" from Barbie Chang. Copyright © 2017
by Victoria Chang. Reprinted with the permission of The Permissions Company,
LLC on behalf of Copper Canyon Press, www.coppercanyonpress.org.

Interior illustrations © Gail Swanlund and Benjamin Weissman.

LIBRARY OF CONGRESS CATALOGING-IN-PUBLICATION DATA
Names: Gerstler, Amy, author.
Title: Index of women / Amy Gerstler.
Description: New York: Penguin Books, 2021. | Series: Penguin poets
Identifiers: LCCN 2020032154 (print) | LCCN 2020032155 (ebook) |
ISBN 9780143136217 (trade paperback) | ISBN 9780525507802 (ebook) |
Subjects: LCSH: Women—Poetry. | LCGFT: Poetry.
Classification: LCC PS3557.E735 I53 2021 (print) | LCC PS3557.E735
(ebook) | DDC 811/.54—dc23
LC record available at https://lccn.loc.gov/2020032154
LC ebook record available at https://lccn.loc.gov/2020032155

Printed in the United States of America

1st Printing

Set in Adobe Garamond Pro • Designed by Catherine Leonardo

For Benjamin Weissman:
you never cease to amaze me

CONTENTS

Women suffer from the loss of a secret once known.

—Joy Williams

. . . thinking she could overcome
being classified thinking

she could be an agent of her own
classification

—Victoria Chang

INDEX of WOMEN

{from an Introduction to some fragments of the Index of Women}

So, given the document's age and ravaged state,
it's far from the epic we thought we'd be left
by our ancestors. Where, for example,
are the gods, floods, beasts, and prophesies?

of these women tell me

In fairness, evidence suggests that the authors
of this scattershot, fragmented volume never
called what they were collecting and setting
down an "epic," "catalog," or "index"
but instead used a term that most closely
translates to "inheritance" in our language.

she who holds the keys
she who can speak to bees
she who guards the crosswalks
she who unites disparate nations and faiths
will remain ageless all her days.

Also uncharacteristic of a true epic is the text's
intrinsic ambivalence, for instance, its mentions,
often ironic, of *modesty, gracefulness, purity, delicacy,*
civility, compliance, reticence, chastity, affability, and
politeness, next to sentences like *"slut" being,*
of course, an honorific, and *when the body insists,*
who are you to contradict it? as well as numerous
other sexual references.

of these women tell me:
such as she, swallower of swords, sorrow, and semen
such as she who is a physical stud
such as she who is born anew every second
such as she who breaks speed limits
such as she who represents the totality of what can be known
such as she who leads mixed-gender teams into battle
she who manages, no matter where she is, to keep herself clean
she who was buried in her Girl Scout uniform—
sash covered with merit badges

Authored over the course of generations,
often under dire conditions (some type
of plague may have been raging
during the first few decades in which
it was written), the text at times seems
to mutate, containing a shifting chorus
of voices singing in unison. At other
times, speakers are for pages
engaged in spirited debates.

we loaded our battered Chevy with provisions:
bedding, bottles, pots, pans, high chair, crib,
then she began having second thoughts about our mission.

Envision, then, a text riddled with disputed
fragments, its breath smelling of cough drops,
mouthwash, and cigarettes, or instant coffee,
or gin, its hands shoved into oven mitts.
A document that comes down to us in tatters,
passages of which we are told were composed
over a Royal Warrior stove in bright brave true blue!!

of these women tell me: superlative examples of their kind

For no reason we can find
the document includes a selection
of cheerful seasonal songs
and several attempts to describe
the sounds made by wind chimes.

Tell me of the seamstress of souls
of those night wanderers and root diggers
of she who moves easily between worlds
she who holds her teacup high over her head
when victorious, laughing so hard
tea splatters down her gown

We had hoped to learn about ancient notions
of the heroic. All we have found so far are vows,
curses, recipes, regrets, prayers, elegies,
love songs, tales of drug trips, protests,
remedies, household hints, and practical
instructions: for growing tomatoes in poor soil,
for curing infections, and for easing the dying
out of this life, to offer three random examples.

a Girl Scout's honor is to be trusted
a Girl Scout is loyal
a Girl Scout is a friend to all and a sister to every other Girl Scout
a Girl Scout is clean in thought, word, and deed

It is impossible to tell when the last undamaged copy was lost.

you are not going to get a wilting flower
you are going to get a hard-charging female

Perhaps it can be loosely classed as a "shattered epic"?

it is recounted that women drove their cars to remote sites
to mate with rivers, animals, and trees

Here the page is badly damaged, with only four lines decipherable:

such as she who could diagnose with her nose
such as she who can say NO
such as she who tends those floating in coma
such as she who sees ghosts before breakfast . . .

Virginity

Lying down on the rug with someone and getting dust
bunnies in your hair. The eloquence of long pauses.
Passing notes rather than speaking. A basement fogged
with pot smoke. Trying to read another body via its breathing.
The idea that if you kiss someone you can taste what they
just ate. Refusing to eat what your mother cooks anymore,
which hurts her feelings. But you can't stand dead sautéed
animal inside your mouth now, so you have to spit it out.
The myth that innocence is protective. The idea of not
being able to stop. Reading secret magazines a cousin stuffed
into the bottom of his sleeping bag. The idea that someone
curious about your body isn't interested in the private theater
of your mind. Theories that there might be a kind of
violence about it. How Mother insists that without true love
it's just worthless humping, and the idea that for the life
you aspire to, she's probably wrong. What your body has
promised for so long. The idea of your disastrous premiere.
The idea of someone laughing at you after. The idea of
hoofprints, stampede damage, being crushed underfoot.
The idea of keeping all this hidden as you slowly lotus open.

Ode to Birth Control

Fertility hot on my heels like a Fury,
and I at that young age in such a blind hurry
to embrace the opposite of what was chaste.
That's where you came in—You jellies,
You douches, in white pliable tubes
like the family toothpaste. And You:
cylindrical plastic applicator, squirting
a plume of contraceptive goo
on a bathroom wall
that first night I fumbled with you.

Ancient birth control methods include:
fish bladders linen sheaths
honey lint acacia leaves
and my personal favorite: *crocodile dung*
gummy substances to stop up
the mouth of the womb
silkworm guts were also thought useful

Margaret Sanger's words
clang in the head:
woman as brood animal

A friend sends a Victorian postcard
of a large stork, bundle dangling from its beak,
chasing a woman in hat and bustle
as she attempts to defend herself with her umbrella.
The caption reads: *and still the villain pursues her*

Rare, that early flash of self-knowledge
that while I might care deeply
for other people's children, I was not mother
material. Not sane enough. Ill too often.
Etc. I don't believe I have to provide an excuse.
And so, You, Madame Diaphragm,
were pressed into service: shallow rubber cup
anointed with cold-as-a-Slurpee spermicide,
then folded in half and shoved up inside.
The diaphragm slept in a pink plastic case
that clicked shut like the hatch of a
spacecraft. Diaphragm: a contraceptive
device that Margaret Sanger (I will kiss her
shoes if we meet in the afterlife) was jailed
for smuggling into the U.S., in brandy
bottles, birth control being illegal in 1918.
Pamphlets or books on the topic were
also banned, considered obscene.

During certain years I nevertheless
ached for an infant's weight to cradle, caress,
longed to clone *in utero* the men I loved best.
Nowadays, when I get my hands on
a nice, juicy baby, somebody's burping,
shitting little god, I tremble and pray.
Some babies wave arms and legs languidly
as if rehearsing water ballet.
A few are as inconsolable as adults.
Except a baby is never wrong.

To be taken over, invaded. To swell. To harbor a being in your body who won't
leave. To be a vessel, a container. To once again become secondary to a life
deemed more important than yours. To host a kind of parasite. To have your

organs squashed to make room for another human. Not to be alone in your body anymore, to become a form of packaging and/or housing. To be temporarily double-souled. To eat, sleep, and breathe for two. To be sapped, waylaid, stopped in your tracks. To be trapped, to have no means of escape, to be forced to

(until men and women are absolved from
the fear of becoming parents,
except when they themselves desire it)

become not a person but a place, a site, someone's ground zero, their very first hometown. They hide in the guest room of your womb and set up camp. And your body begins to shift for their benefit. Whether you're willing or not. Whether you have money or a place to live. Whether you can take of yourself, or

These "medicines," these devices,
became in my day as part of one's anatomy,
one's exertions/insertions,
the secrecy of secretions,
the panics, narrow escapes,
nightmares of being chased
by armies of greedy babies.
Let me alone! Forgive me!
We girls stared down pharmacy clerks
or squirmed in stirrups
of bow tie–wearing gynecologists,
bought or begged these items
and prayed they'd work.

or, you may eat a concoction of oil and quicksilver after the fact

And You IUDs . . . Copper-7, tiny
wire-wrapped numeral who caused
a year of hellish cramps. Dalkon
Shield shaped like a horseshoe crab.
Hormone pills in roulette wheel dispensers.

Plastic, rubber, and chemical protectresses,
all I have to offer is this awkward song.
Across the trajectory of my childless life,
I call out to you now, name you and praise you.
I owe you all I've tried to be.

Anthem

Dear blitzkrieg of wetness and breasts.
Dear masseuses and muses, thighs sluiced
with juices. Dear coven members posing
peppery questions, like: *Is a witchy third breast
akin to a third eye?* Can we climb into the light
now from cellars and attics? Can we abandon
our nectar dance temporarily, stop skimming
froth off cauldrons and let our bravura arias
ascend? So much depends upon shrewd,
ingenious, difficult women, prodigal daughters
and wisecracking wives, unwilling brides, bakers
of exploding pies, giantesses in whose tresses
condors nest, audacious maidens with blood on
their tongues, all of whose chests house untamed
hearts: How is it your beauty never departs?

Tooth Fairy Sonnet

I can't tolerate daylight, so I slip into the dim of kids'
bedrooms at night, adorned with necklaces made of
baby teeth. The color white makes me retch. I'd like
to resign, become something other than a fang
collector. I can fly, but only as a limp, boneless ghost,
a spectral jellyfish with floating skirts, a marble quarry
whirlwind. I smell of chalk dust, old dental records,
ossuaries, loss, and skeletons cleaned of meat. My
breath is a whiff of extinction. I have eyes like
mustard seeds. No, I'm not pretty. To reach your
world of porcelain drinking fountains and molar-
rotting toffees, I navigate a long, winding tunnel
each evening, parts of which are dark, and parts
of which are the hurt pink of a sore throat.

An Aging Opera Singer Speaks at Her First AA Meeting

Once I got sober god quit speaking to me.
I miss her strenuously. She was an alto.
Her speech was aria. I'm a soprano. Renée
Fleming says sopranos are happy in operas
for the first five minutes and then it all falls
apart. For better or worse I have tumbled
into love numerous times due to a caramelly
melt or satisfying rasp in someone's voice.
In religion I am equally vulnerable. Sei
Shōnagon says priests must be handsome
or no one will like to be pious. Good looks
have affected me less than lovely song
or talk. I like to ride vocal breakers, waves
that flow invisibly yet powerfully out of
the mouth and can carry you for what I'd
assumed would be forever. *Are your sins merely
fears?* my god would whisper, adding, *Why this
craving for forgiveness?* Of course, I had no reply.
Why is sobriety so harrowing? So lonely?
Why can't it become some kind of high note,
a fabulous flowering? What wouldn't I trade
to be able to bathe in forgiveness, to wade
in and splash around like I did one summer
in a lake upstate, unafraid of how I looked
in a bathing suit because I was young and
humming to myself like a bird and drunk
on my own voice, its possibilities, range,
and sweetness, or the mirage of my future
or who I thought might next wish to kiss me.

Back then I'd stride into a bar and rows
of backlit bottles would throw their gemlike
glow my way, gamely standing in for sacred
flames or a tossed bouquet. Patrons sat
on padded stools, or eased into booths
which swallowed them slowly, like pythons.
People stirred their drinks with fingers or
swizzle sticks or toothpicks on which olives were
uncomplainingly impaled. Conversations grew
legible in cryptic bits. On the muted TV bolted
to the wall in one corner, football players traded
concussions. Paintings of generations of bulldogs,
successive pets of a long-gone proprietor, adorned
one wall. After several cocktails, letters might
appear on a curtain like chalk on a blackboard,
a definitive voice in cursive, instructive, insistent,
as that curtain fluttered, winglike, on its brass rings.
Now even that voice has gone silent. Don't stop me
if you've heard this one before, just listen harder.
A washed-up warbler walked into a bar yesterday,
she being me, hoping to sit in the dark and let
fragments of chatter, human talk-song loosened
by booze, wash over her. She saw mouths moving
but could hear no sound. I consider this a brutal
kind of exile. Everything veers away from me now.
Where is the victory here? This is what I want to
know: What are you all going to do to forgive me,
to revive that voice in my ear (it sometimes seemed
to emanate from my left temple) and save me?

To a Head of Lettuce

May I venture to address you, vegetal friend?
A lettuce is no less than me, so I respect you,
though it's also true I may make a salad of you
later. That's how we humans roll. Our species
is blowing it, big-time, as you no doubt know,
dependent as you are on water and soil
we humans pollute. You're a *crisphead*,
an iceberg lettuce, scorned in days of yore
for being mostly fiber and water. But new
research claims you've gotten a bad rap,
that you're more nutritious than we knew.
Juicy and beautiful, your leaves can be used
as tortillas. If I peer through a lettuce leaf,
the view takes on the translucent green
of the newest shoots. Sitting atop your pile,
next to heaps of radicchio, you do seem
a living head, a royal personage who should
be paid homage. I am not demanding to be
reassured. I just want to know what you know,
what you think your role is—and hear what you
have to say about suffering long denied, the wisdom
of photosynthesis, stages of growth you've passed
through. I can almost hear your voice as I pay
for you at the cash register, a slightly gravelly sound,
like Kendrick Lamar's voice, or early Bob Dylan,
both singers of gruff poetic truth. Nothing less
was expected from you, sister lettuce, nothing less.

Dead Butterfly

dead empress of winged things
weightless flake of flight
you rest in state on my desk
more delicate and flatter than
this scrap of foolscap you lie on
flatter even than my dad's voice
when he was mad   like death
anger drained him of color
but his temper was gentle
flare-ups were rare
and of course   nonexistent now
since he was found
lifeless in bed   a cut on his head
how did he make it down the hall
do you think after he fell? homing instinct?
the undersides of your wings
have elongated spots
silver iridescences whose shapes
vary like globs of oil floating on water
your three visible legs
are tiny whiskers slightly curved
your head a majestic black seed
I fetch my magnifying glass
to view your life form
so difficult to glimpse
except fleetingly while in motion
for twelve days I have selfishly kept you
for private study on a corner of my desk
you seem a saint
remaining uncorrupt   obligingly intact

perhaps your oranges yellows and blacks
are imperceptibly dimming
but I can't see it yet   you look fresh
I long to pet you but know
you would crumble to dust
like pollen on my fingertips
dead monarch will you ferry
my dead father a missive in which I admit
he was right about everything:
my cousin's sham marriage
and 9/11   about how one should never eat
a loveless meal   about craving more time
alive   about the eternity of our ends?

Viennese Pathology Museum

With their vast lawns and lordly trees wielding floral authority, the grounds make one feel small. At least they did me. Housed in a squat, rotund tower of dun-colored brick built in 1784, the museum had once been a jail for the insane, chains still attached to the walls in small, dark cells with barred doors. Exhibits are shelved in the old cells. The word "dungeon" fits well, though the building's politely described in guidebooks as "fortress-like." From outside, the tower looks like a giant bran muffin. This resemblance led to a German word for "cake" becoming slang for "mental asylum." Five stories high, the ex-nuthouse/museum could be mistaken for an ancient observatory. The building's ringed by rows of vertical slits, which, since windows read as eyes, give it a sinister look. Visitors climb stone stairs between floors. That summer I was twenty, all I thought about was the great river of suffering, meaning my own.

Large specimen jars are what I recall, contents suspended like plums in heavy syrup. And how cold and dark the building felt, earlier centuries' air sifting into one's lungs, tainting one's brain. Only the jars seemed lit, by murky brown beams, like sun through muddy water. Lightheaded with dread, I wanted to flee as soon as I'd entered. Yet the museum seemed a test I had to pass by remaining, despite growing faint, to stare at a room of jarred infants, each representing some birth defect. Was this what came of procreation? Why was their fate not mine and vice versa? Did the specimens in glass canisters cry out, however inaudibly, from their formaldehyde naps? How long had these babies been sleeping? Was theirs a heavenly rest—bloated, alone (Siamese twins the sole exception)—each afloat in his own final solution, unable to say if something itched or hurt? A greenish fetus, junior mermaid, embraced her tail. Suffering seemed to drip from the stone enclosure as molasses trickles down walls of old sugar refineries.

A tourist, nursing twenty words of German, afraid everyone could tell I was a Jew, I also felt tugs of connection to Vienna. My grandparents on my father's side had come from Austria. People eating pastry in cafés and walking avenues of linden trees looked like me, so much so that I was often asked directions, by other tourists, or even natives in their rapid-fire German. No help at all, I was happy to lend my laminated map, which I flapped at askers like some kind of stiff flag. I was able only to order *Kaffee mit Milch* and say *Entschuldigung* when I bumped into locals, which I frequently did, forgetting I had arms and legs to keep track of, alive only in the furious hive of my head, wondering if the bees in there would ever learn to get along or make honey. Was the pathology museum an endurance test? A shove toward *Schadenfreude*, toward embracing the fate of this mortal coil, always in mind, never yet faced?

I wouldn't mind getting back the complexion or energy I had in those days. But you couldn't pay me to re-inhabit that younger, seething, bottled-up self. *Decay and chaos await you*, something with bat guano breath kept telling me, and I would drink, smoke, or kiss anything to reduce the volume of that constant hissing. Getting older has helped, I guess. At twenty, I ran down the stone stairs of the Viennese pathology museum and burst into the park. For an hour or so, I lay on my back in manicured grass, waiting for the tour to end and my friends to exit. Breathing carefully, like I had just learned how, I opened my eyes every few minutes on blinding brightness to watch chickadees flit. It's hardly ever like that now. But in the pathology museum I was ashamed and afraid of being found out, or of waking up floating and ravenous in some dusty jar.

Crystal Blue Persuasion

why is the light always retreating?
am I drugged enough yet?
secrets erupt from the crown of my head
and tongues wag in the trees
but no matter how long I stay away
a watch gets kept over my body
from way up in god's penthouse
where constant recitations take place
to keep the virtuous safe
nonetheless when not high
I can't feel blessings drizzle down
the designs in god's mind
are tweaked then deleted
my quiet refusals
my exquisite little inklings
my high-minded reliance
on exact research terms
my pious recitals take me only so far
whereas fruity cocktails
smoldering joints bombard
my sorry heart
which barely beats
without chemical help
a soggy paper boat that heart
on the brink of sinking
into the burbling river
you get ferried across when ready
to *pass over* meaning *pass away* meaning
Charon rows you, fearsome rower I bet

so you pep pills you bitter soporifics
strive diligently / work consciously
gift me with forbidden images
with illusions I'm fire-minded
that I glow and that mightily entwined
you and I and this high even exist

Glimpse

Faces loom and eclipse under heaven's attentive glare.
Hieroglyph eyebrows. Burnished cheek. Dark scribble
of beard. He wants to know: *How far can you see into me
by the roar of this morning's light?* The surface of his lips
like the thirsty surface of sandstone or granite. *Am I
becoming statuary?* he asks. *Then let me be monument.*
Long ago, we'd read every pore on a face.
We'd feel groundwater surge beneath our bare
feet. We'd sniff each other's penumbras, judge
friend or foe by aroma, as mice and deer do.
Today, light collects in the folds of our clothes, sloshes
in pockets. Light is gilding his kinky corona of hair.
Is it permissible to kiss him? Most people kiss with
their eyes closed, irises silvering behind their lids.
Even as bodies are lapped by encroaching black,
a light may develop out of events. In the end,
that's what we pray for: a room lit by small lamps,
body laid out on the table, washed and gleaming
like ebony. We imbibe his rich shadow. Milky light
showers down through skylights and we guzzle
that too, open mouths glowing like kilns. His gaze
that of a man aware he's being looked at, though his
eyes seem fixed on something far off in the distance.

Gender Is Fluid

Some nights I wanted
to be the shover
the pummeler
the battering ram
not the open door
open legs
gooey femmy receptacle
I needed to know
what it felt like
to say *I fucked her*
or *I'll fuck anything*
that moves I wanted
to push in deep
feel gripped
tightened around
so I could better know
my shape
be spelunker
not spelunkee

In dreams I almost
accomplished this
but didn't know
what it was like to be **HARD**,
and therefore ultimately
wasn't,
wilted straightaway
because I couldn't
properly imagine it

Unconsummated straining
was all I got in those dreams
when I wanted so badly
to spill into her and drip
down later between her legs
hot broth shot off
in the dark
short-lived rocketing
then be slammed (as though
a cartoon anvil had dropped
on my head) into sleep

Night Life

How can this equal rest or peace, this garble of gasps, snuffles, and horse-like snorts? His lips flutter as though he's blowing bubbles, his moans so choked he must be drowning . . . or are his legs being sucked in by quicksand, the way a restaurant critic sucks the bones of her osso buco? In my overheated, nightgowned silence I watch him flinch in a puddle of bedside light. A range of ages and plights wash over his face. Who is this sleeping, unshaven male, this slab of snoring meat, this leaky ship of divinity? I stare across the chasm which divides each waking or sleeping creature, whether they've touched each other or not. He's a magician who made an orchard disappear, an unhinged shooter from St. Louis, a plum-colored shadow, a handful of chameleon teeth, one of god's toboggans, a tree denuded of leaves bleeding beads of amber.

How Happy I Was When Mother Bought Me Those Three Dresses

They don't make dresses like that anymore. Not like when I was a girl, in Europe. Hand-stitched, lined with silk. High-waisted or drapey. Moiré, rose, and midnight blue. I'd give anything to see those dresses again. To rub my fingers across the little embroidered jackets we wore over them. We emigrated so young, my cousin and I, and all by ourselves. She hit it big in Hollywood during the fifties. When her first movie opened at Cannes, you wouldn't believe the limousine traffic. Years after the war, visiting Vienna with my new husband, I pretended I didn't know what the old man in the bathing cap shouted in German. Shriveled and paunchy, towel tucked around his waist, he pointed at me and yelled: "Get out of the pool, Jew, you're polluting the water!" Two attendants rushed up and suggested he leave, tugging his arms, but he planted his feet on the tile and kept yelling. I floated easily on the water's surface while the attendants removed him. When I climbed out of the pool everyone stared. I was wet and golden-haired, young and pretty back then, taking my time drying myself. The other swimmers stood in the shallow end, silent. You could hear the water lapping and gurgling. I never went back to that swim club. Every December in America, my children had a Christmas tree. One bank account I keep hidden, in case I need to disappear. Am I, in ways I can't see, unclean? Who is this trapped in me, Jonah imprisoned in his whale, a small girl on an ocean liner, refusing to speak, surrounded by people who don't know German, hands clapped over her ears? Tonight, I'll pick my way down the cliff where my pretty house sits, to the ocean's foamy lip. As I soak the torn garments of my body, I'll pray: May the waves fade these stains.

Storing Up

It will not hold, this whipstitch of peace,
this clock-tick of calm, this brief release
when no one's sick in this house,
and there's a mood of safekeeping,
when no one's pounding the wall or weeping.

Vivid and fleeting the moments flow
(a trite thought from several hours ago . . .)
Someone yawns. Someone else hacks and rasps.
But it's nothing. All's well,
though this will not last:

that for now all the floors are swept,
and the animals fed and the Sabbath kept,
and the meal eaten, leftovers tucked away,
and the world's chaos held at bay,
and those made sleepy by eating put warmly to bed

their heads facing east . . . no, it will not last,
this moment of peace. Yet if the Earth keeps
twirling, as I trust that she may,
could this blip of grace live in me
if I don't scare it away?

Buried Song

When our love first became alien to me,
when you first peered at me like I was smeared
and illegible, then a rude-humored voice
started to leak from some objects, a tube of anise
toothpaste, for example, a taste I can't sanction
given licorice's near-opiate sweetness,
so like that of a well-told lie. So I questioned
the right of that toothpaste, and later a lamp,
to disparage me. But that was as far as I got
in defending myself. There's something crushing
about being judged by the butter knife you just
buttered your muffin with. When I took issue
with its critique, I was met by aggressive
metallic laughter. How long have objects been
nursing these grievances? Though the authority
they seized seemed like a disease, I was nonetheless
hurt by what they implied. This winter, while seated
beneath a chestnut tree, trying to unite my mind
long enough to understand a paragraph, the tree
spoke to me, though I at first mistook its voice
for tuba music, a rake scraping flagstone, or
someone snaking a drain. Though the tree
astonished me with its equanimity, though it talked
gently about how to treat ailments not easily named,
when I left the tranquil courtyard that afternoon and
ran smack into you and you looked at me askance,
it took several days to recover from your glance.

My Ego

is a dented suit of armor, a designer gown
with grimy lining. She's the cause of false beliefs.
She fucks up my ability to love. She's prickly
and tender as an artichoke heart. She proposes
to me so frequently I can't hear other people
speak. She's a self-anointed guide who materializes
at my side with a flourish of trumpets and a bullhorn.
She's a forged love letter, a jailer impersonating a
friend. She's a series of flashbacks in which I'm
both victim and hero. I try to bribe her into exile,
but she calls herself my servant and falls weeping
at my feet. I'm forever banishing her, this mistress
of disguises, even as she clambers back into my lap,
begging my pardon and getting all kissy with me,
grabbing my hand and jamming it down her blouse.

Letters from a Lost Doll

Among the lost manuscripts of Franz Kafka are some letters from a doll, written to an unknown girl. Kafka had encountered the girl while walking in a park in Berlin in 1923, in the company of Dora Diamant, his last companion. The child was weeping in despair at the loss of her doll. He talked with her. Unhesitating, he told her that the doll was not lost, but traveling. She had sent him a letter. Consoled but still suspicious, the girl insisted on seeing the letter. Kafka went home and composed it, bringing the page next day to the park, and continuing over a few weeks to frame further letters.

—Kenneth Gross, in the introduction to *On Dolls*

October, 1964

Dearest One,

Pardon me for having taken a while to write you. There has been much to think about, and I was unaccustomed to being or thinking alone, without your presiding, abiding presence filling my consciousness like snow. I had to get my head working in an unprecedented way. I had to dig fresh thought-channels. I did not know this would be necessary, and it has been a lot of work. Now that there is some distance between us, due to this accident that has befallen me, I'd like to take the opportunity to ask you some questions, beginning with this: What is the nature of the bond between us? Now that we are parted, I hope temporarily, I find myself in an increasingly philosophical cast of mind, and so am moved to ask: What am I to you and you to me?

I know well how we began. At Christmas several years ago, you lifted me from my coffin-like box with the cellophane window in its lid. You held me in your arms, tight against your chest, as though you'd just given birth to me. Your eyes were wet, as they so often were back then. Your gaze awakened me. You began to touch me in ways both tentative and knowing, awkward and sure, forgetting your other Christmas presents, those you'd opened, and the toys still wrapped in silver paper. Whenever you held me after that, we comprised a secret society of two. Pressed into your ribs during turbulent nights, I was with you as you groaned and tried to cry out from a sleep-clogged throat. We were inseparable.

Fast-forward to the present. As we sat on that bench in the park by the lake last week, how did I manage to fall through that gap between the bench back and the seat slats and get lost? Did you drop me accidentally? Did I slide from your grip on purpose? And if so, to what end? Here the geese sleep on that tiny man-made island in the middle of the lake, heads tucked under their wings. At night the trees hum songs in a language so ancient it predates birdsong. Another question: Were you my god or was I yours? Was I your child or you mine? I really want to know.

Sincerely,
Your Doll

November, 1964

My Dear Child,

What do I miss from my life with you? Mutual adoration and worship? Holding the office of sacred object? The times you tried to feed me gingerbread? The richness of an almost erotic safety conferred by citizenship in our private world? Waiting out your measles and fevers? I loved being confined to bed with you after you had your tonsils out and couldn't speak for a week—or refused to—inhabiting in tandem your hot, furious silence.

I miss sitting in a place of honor on the pile of pillows at the head of your nicely made bed, alongside the small red plush horse who smelled of the clean sawdust he was stuffed with and whose saddle was edged with gold thread. I miss the smiling green stuffed alligator with the kink in his tail. Also, the white felt mouse with red bead eyes who squeaked when squeezed. Innocent-looking though she may be, that mouse is capable of being quite sarcastic.

I confess that there were things about our life together I do not miss, events that in fact I recall with hints of nausea or spurts of fury. For example, the times you balanced me on the rim of the tub while you were bathing. This was a practice your mother warned you against repeatedly, yet you ignored her. Predictably, I would sometimes fall into the tub, causing the fabric of my dress to bleed magenta tendrils into the hot water, a process which so fascinated you the first few times it happened that it took you nearly a minute of staring to register that I needed immediate rescue. Each time this occurred you were scolded by your mother as she attempted to dry me and set me right. Sharply, she declared you were on the road to ruining me. But this is something I try to push out of my mind.

Equally painful is the memory, admittedly dating from when you were younger, of the day you experimented with using me to tease the family cat. Suffice it to say that even at that tender age, once those dreadful claws had caught in my hair you realized the peril and ceased this beastly sport. But why dwell on these few echoes of the downside of our love? For I do miss the life I led with you, mostly indoors but sometimes carried into the car, or onto playgrounds or to your grandmother's house. It's true that our life together seems increasingly unreal to me now: the waffle weave of the dark blue curtains in your room, which at certain hours admitted light as through a sieve, stippling your coverlet with what looked like sparks. The other bed in your room belongs to your little sister, rough with toys, always drooling, whom I do not miss. A manic child who sleeps little, she was always in motion. Immediately after learning to walk she learned to run, albeit in that stumbling, drunken way toddlers have of ambulating.

I also miss the wooden giraffe coat rack in your room. Your cough medicine on the night table in winter in a brown-tinted bottle, flanked by a glass and sticky spoon. Sometimes you'd drop berries in the lap of my dress, telling me they were apples. They were a perfect size for doll apples, and almost the right color. I miss my conversations with your whirlwind little sister's more babyish toys: blocks, rattles, genial plush bears wearing garish bow ties who never had a bad word to say about anyone. I miss the mysteries contained by the closet you and your sister shared: a hiding and sulking place, portal to other realities. I miss your terror of the grating sound crickets make, and how I was able to comfort you in the throes of that panic. The fact that my love could always soothe you was vital to me. When will I be lifted up again by your little hands?

Truly,
Your Doll

December, 1964

Dear Child,

I am not the first doll to write letters to her little girl. Not at all. There was a famous writer who wrote in German . . . he died in 1924 but when he was alive, he served as eager intermediary for such a correspondence. And there have been others. But back to you and me.

As mentioned in my last letter, I took such pride in being your solace, your protector, the one who went everywhere with you, perhaps even shared hidden provinces of your mind. I logged more intimate hours with you than even your parents. Over time, a ferocity welled up in me as I became a kind of shield, banishing your fears, especially at night. Just by being hugged and clutched by you, I could step into the role of vanquisher of your pain or sorrow. I could even cool your anger. From the first, I had such a bottomless hunger to comfort you.

But had I become a less effectual protector of late? Were you, as more of your birthday parties sped by, increasingly haunted by the fears of an older child, complicated worries that even the most devoted doll has little power to dispel? By tumbling through the slats of that park bench, was I withdrawing my waning protection of you, just as you began to find it less potent and to desire more sophisticated defenses and protections? These anxieties on my part, about being outgrown, ballooned to the point where I sometimes felt jealous of other toys and amusements you began to favor. Jigsaw puzzles, for example, or your butterfly collection in that flat glass box. Or the elaborately dressed flamenco dancer figurine your grandmother brought back from Spain, feet glued to a stand the size of a silver dollar, tiny castanets sewn to her hands. These fears keep leading me to wonder: Was I shed, or did I flee? Or did I slip away in a mutual parting we were both only half-conscious of?

"Leaving is the bravest and finest act of all," a fellow wanderer once observed. I am a newcomer to freedom, to having my own way, and I feel a dark giddiness rising within me. Since you lost me of course there's a feeling of exile, perhaps even intimations of death, but also a surge of wild possibilities, new beginnings. My dress has gotten a bit soiled, my braids mussed, but I believe these are small sacrifices to be embraced as honors, as medals if you will, bespeaking my newly heightened state. Is this my time for experiment and action? My time to conquer?

Many Fond Regards,
Your Favorite

P.S. How is it that I would only come alive when you touched or spoke to me, and otherwise I lay dazed, empty, inert? Am I experiencing a second awakening?

Possibly February (?), 1965

Little Girl,

Will I find my way back to you someday, wiser, fuller, neither of us looking foolish or losing face, ready to start afresh and abide in constant acknowledgment of the wildness of being alive and the blessed rarity of love? Since we parted, sometimes at night I am seized by a strange desire to suffer, to drag my physical self into deprivation and dirt so that I might learn and become both exalted and humbled. Ants make rude comments about me as they file by in formation, but being well bred, I ignore them. They are but soldiers en route to another field of battle. Dogs snuffle me but leave me mostly alone. So far, I have had to endure only one rain, which was short-lived. Luckily, being made mostly of cotton with a durable plastic head, I dried quickly with minimal wrinkling. One hot day it got pretty lizardy, but lizards show no interest in me, skittering after little insects and baby snails, and of course chasing each other.

Untethered from you, I find I am absolute master of the sky above me, and the ground on which I rest, tickled by wisps of grass. Solitude and freedom are spinning within me, gathering strength like a storm. You have given me an incredible gift, perhaps the greatest favor you could have done me. I am extremely grateful. Yes, my empire here is an intangible one, for my enjoyment and domination of it are only things of the spirit. Yet it is into that realm that I find myself more and more forcefully drawn every day. A little earth has gotten into my mouth as the days have passed, and to my surprise, it tastes sweet.

Best Wishes,
An Emancipated Doll

Poof

Here on my lap, in a small plastic bag,
my share of your ashes. Let me not squander
them. Your family blindsided me with this gift.
We want to honor your bond they said at the end
of your service, which took place, as you'd
arranged, in a restaurant at the harbor,
an old two-story boathouse made of dark
wood. Some of us sat on the balcony, on black
leather bar stools, staring at rows of docked boats.
Both your husbands showed up and got along.
And, of course, your impossibly handsome son.
After lunch, a slideshow, and testimonials,
your family left to toss their share of you
onto the ocean, along with some flowers.

You were the girlfriend I practiced kissing
with in sixth grade during zero-sleep
sleepovers. You were the pretty one.
In middle school I lived on Diet Coke and
your sexual reconnaissance reports. In this
telling of our story your father never hits
you or calls you a whore. Always gentle
with me, he taught me to ride a bike after
everyone said I was too klutzy to learn.
In this version we're not afraid of our bodies.
In this fiction, birth control is easy to obtain,
and never fails. You still dive under a stall
divider in a restroom at the beach to free me
after I get too drunk to unlock the door. You still
reveal the esoteric mysteries of tampons. You

still learn Farsi and French from boyfriends
as your life ignites. In high school I still guide you
safely out of the stadium when you start yelling
that the football looks amazing as it shatters
into a million shimmering pieces, as you
loudly admit that you'd dropped acid.

We lived to be sixty. Then poof, you vanished.
I can't snort you, or dump you out over my head,
coating myself in your dust like some hapless cartoon
character who's just blown herself up, yet remains
unscathed, as is the way in cartoons. In this version,
I remain in place for a while. Did you have a good
journey? I'm still lagging behind, barking up all
the wrong trees, whipping out my scimitar far
in advance of what the occasion demands. As I
drive home from your memorial, you fizz in
my head like a distant radio station. What
can I do to bridge this chasm between us?
In this fiction, I roll down the window, drive
uncharacteristically fast. I tear your baggie
open with my teeth and release you at 85
miles an hour, music cranked up full blast.

Earth, Temple, Gods

A woman's feet, in lace-up sandals made of stone.
Her centuries-old long stone toes. How can
toes be so eloquent, evoking love and something
akin to pity? Snaking down her back, between
her shoulder blades, a long-looped braid,
entwined with ribbons and flowers, also carved
marble. The braid's woven stone patience.
A mineral smell. Sounds of dripping. Glimpses
of waiting fates, of young, vulnerable mankind,
staring from time-whitened statues' eyes.

The centuries slippery as spilled milk during
coronavirus confinement. *We're all monks now*
one monk joked in a Catholic newsletter I glanced
at online. Maybe time melts when one's confined
to quarters, staring at photos of beautiful ruins,
statues sans noses, some with only half a face, each
looking as though, despite losses and griefs, she
might speak. And me so restless and unnerved today,
dying to hear what these long-gone women could say,
looking for any place to rest my frightened eyes.

Translation

a rising stroke   a falling stroke
a crooked form   a hooked stroke

this character means
one who's sexually ambidextrous

what some claim are characters
taken from the Chinese
others believe to be lifted
from the secret language of women

those Sanskrit words are cauldrons
containing gallon upon gallon
of simmering history

"loves," "anticipates," "believes," and "longs for"
as well as variations of such words and expressions
will not be considered
as binding or having any mutually agreed-upon meaning
at all

or maybe it was just more untranslated
terrorist chatter?

individual words and letters
become extinct
no one uses that consonant anymore
so drop it before you humiliate yourself

a secret language
only women could read
what did these females
privately write to each other?
what lore was handed down?
The Girl Who Saved a Fort
Sojourner Truth's Youth
Joan of Arc Didn't Die in That Fire!
The Untold Story of Lady Godiva
Florence Nightingale, Saboteur
The Tomboy Who Tamed a Nation

this verb means *to travel for the purpose of improving one's health*
this noun means *a present brought back from a perilous journey*

she feels like a series of hesitantly drawn characters
vibrating imperceptibly on the page, with meanings like:
a grain afloat on the ocean or
go ahead, nibble away like a minnow or engulf like a whale, I'm ready to be
ingested

the Chinese word "lin" has a range of meanings
not exhausted by any single word of another language

this dictionary is arranged according to the number of strokes
required to draw the characters
those with fewest strokes coming first

this character means *a man allergic to kindness*
these two characters mean *the mouthpiece of a hookah*

here we have a quiescent vowel
shy as a kid on her first day of school

the dazzling anger of the belittled has its own language
the jagged language of the jilted
the skinny-fingered language of plant roots
entwining deep underground
a notation developed to record the hum
of insects' vegetal intentions
the burble of wood nymphs, draped in rain
set down in an alphabet
composed of little images of trees

the alphabet's letters are my tribe
and I mean to live quietly among them
bending my body into meaningful shapes
perhaps entangled with yours
using our whole persons to confess
what can't be, by any other means,
comprehended or expressed

The Semmelweis Opera

In the Semmelweis opera I'll write, there should be no splashing of fake blood onstage. Instead, bolts of red satin will unfurl between the legs of actresses playing women in childbirth.

I get my best ideas while sweeping. The repetitive motion soothes the mind. Sweeping almost mimics synaptic action. Charles Sherrington discovered the synapse, in case you wanted to know. *Sweep, sweep,* the mind leaps. *Sweep, sweep,* chemicals clear the gap between one thought and another, hurtling over the abyss between.

Where I come from, I was a doctor's wife. Never mind what kind of doctor. Never mind what kind of uprising caused his demise and how I ended up here, celebrated in this neighborhood for hazelnut cheesecakes, lamb chops with grapes, plum crumble. Dear Mr. Famous Composer, I am writing to you because I saw the photo in the newspaper of you at the White House with President Truman. Who knew Truman was musical? But the article said he had been a concert pianist in his former life. And if you're good enough for Truman, you're good enough for me. I hope you'll agree that my idea for the Semmelweis opera is too good to waste, like the leftovers of my brisket, braised first in a mixture of olive oil and butter, then cooked slow all day, on a bed of potatoes, carrots, celery root, whole heads of garlic, onion, and parsnips.

It is a good thing that, loud as they are, no one in this household can hear my thoughts.

The doctor I work for came home from the hospital today furious because a patient called him a "health care provider." "I went to medical school," he yelled. "I'm a goddamned physician!" He likes me to address him as Dr. Clark, so I do. He is nice enough, a good father, and crazy about my cooking. His wife can hardly boil noodles. She seems afraid of the stove. But Dr. Clark thinks he knows everything. And know-it-alls do not make breakthroughs. They do not surprise themselves and the world. They are not top doctors. The best show deference to what they are dealing with. They must be in awe of disease and mortality. They must respect these forces. In Sherlock Holmes stories, which helped me learn English, Holmes has incredible respect for his enemy, Professor Moriarty. He's almost in love with him. Holmes's saddest hour is when Moriarty is killed, because then he is truly alone in the world. There are no more equal opponents for him. Oh, how he mourns. Doctors cannot be macho and think they will arm wrestle people's illnesses and win. Even in the kitchen you give your ingredients their due. You have to respect their powers, their indelible natures, their ingenuity, their insistence on being what they are. You cannot think you will dominate them, turn them entirely to your will, break them, or conquer them. This is imperialism, not the spirit of science, or of cooking for that matter. Semmelweis did not have that kind of arrogance. He had the spirit of humility, of questing, of curiosity, of inquiry. This is what makes brilliant scientific minds. This is a key ingredient of genius.

If you try to rush a chocolate soufflé cake, if you don't respect your ingredients (this cake is one of Dr. Clark's favorites, he does not believe in "health food"), you will likely scramble your egg yolks by adding them when the melted chocolate is still too hot. Then there's nothing to do but throw away the mess of chocolate scrambled eggs, which even a dim child won't eat, they taste so terrible. You have no choice but to start over.

When Dr. Clark's children ask me if I have any kids, I tell them the same thing, in exactly the same English words, every time. They ask me this about twice a month as though they have amnesia. I say, "Not everyone is blessed with children." I do not tell them what happened to my babies, nor am I honest about my last name, or what my religion is.

In the Semmelweis opera there will be giant slides projected on a white backdrop at the rear of the stage showing blowups of the organisms that caused childbed fever, slayer of so many women, which Semmelweis's methods later all but prevented. He was the father of modern ideas of antiseptics. He championed washing your hands between patients, maybe even with bleach, instead of being stupid and going straight from cutting up cadavers to delivering babies, your hands a zoo of communicable germs. Dr. Semmelweis's colleagues routinely did this, which killed their patients in droves. They didn't know better. It was accepted practice. Handwashing was beneath their dignity. Idiots. Doctors in Semmelweis's time mocked him for his disinfection campaign. They shamed him. Drummed him out of the profession. Drove him to an early grave. My husband idolized Semmelweis, who died a long time ago, in 1865. Dr. Clark, my employer, Mr. Knows-Everything, had never heard of Semmelweis.

I know what it's like not to be listened to. I know what it's like to be right in hindsight, but at the time everyone laughs and calls you crazy and then it's too late. I know what it's like for once in your life to be the madwoman seeing truth, saying: we have to get our passports and leave.

In the Semmelweis opera I'm writing, a choir of sweet-voiced, naked children whose mothers did not die in childbirth (thanks to Semmelweis) will sing him back to life from the dead. At the close of act three, the soul of Semmelweis will be led onstage by a trio of boys crowned with flowers. Semmelweis will act shyly. His little chaperones will help the doctor onto a fake cloud. Then the four of them will ascend into heaven (really the upper rigging of the theater). This is the reverse of something I once saw done in a production of *The Magic Flute*. Three boys floated down from the ceiling in a basket singing, "We wise spirit boys will guide you / always beside you." So that's how the Semmelweis opera will end, except my three boys and Semmelweis will rise into the rafters singing something cheerful and stirring. What, I don't know. I haven't written it yet.

The Feminine Art of Quilting

As his family slept, Abe Lincoln sat up late,
stitching quilts with a thimble his mother
had given him. Mark Twain stuffed his
snipped-off chest hair into quilts for filler,
which is why, to this day, they are swelteringly
warm. Several fine examples of Escoffier's
"lasagna quilts," with their tomato-sauce-red
batting, can be seen at a special exhibition
at the Louvre. Louis Armstrong wrapped
his horns in trumpet-sized quilts he made
for that purpose. An ancient quilt of blue-green
silk, spattered with blood, was definitively
attributed to Genghis Khan. James Bond's
favorite quilt patterns are "Bow Tie" and
"Mix Me a Martini." Al Capone kept
dropping cigar ash, burning holes in
the quilt he would finish in Alcatraz.
George Washington Carver's quilt woven
entirely of peanut fibers is embroidered with
Bible verses and owned by the Smithsonian.
Hercules quilted between each of his great
labors. He said it helped him unwind.

Horizontal Women

Women free-falling or overcome. Arms raised
or flung. Women mostly young and unsung. Women
diving for pearls. A girl tossing her curls, or out cold
mid-clinch. One muddy gal asleep in a ditch. Women
leaping or snoring. Prone women imploring. A babe
brainy as any female could get. A woman who doesn't
know she's pregnant yet, lying on dry grass awaiting
hard rain. Women in pain. A broad with braceleted
wrists. A chick who insists she won't stand up till
you kiss her. A sister you'd never guess would get
herself murdered. A woman unheard who just lies
there and cries. A femme who mightily sighs.
Woman as some kind of horizon, another woman's hand
at the back of her head. Or, instead, each *she* is the line
at the farthest place you can see, if you squint your eyes,
where the sky seems to descend to touch land or sea.

Art History

Woman with flowered skirt
woman with squirming ermine
woman with squirrels in her purse

woman with figs
woman with mandolin
woman with dustbin

woman with goose eggs
woman with ducks and drakes
woman with scythe and rakes

woman with lark
woman with harp
woman with bite marks

woman with stuffed bear
woman with confetti in her hair
woman with dark stare

woman with mink stole
woman with open kimono
woman with snow globes

woman with list of demands
woman with slapped ass
woman with chapped hands

woman with unpaid bills
woman with oil spill
woman with nitroglycerin pills

woman with severed head
woman with cigarette
woman with flickery TV set and unmade bed

woman with fish baskets on dock
woman with red cock
woman with pterodactyl skeleton

    and walkie-talkie and large coffee

My Late Wife

Does it surprise you to learn that I once had a wife?
Someone to whom I showed my wounds, who made me
dangerous because, at unstrung moments with her, I was
so happy? It's not something I talk easily about. She vowed
to help me get my fate straight, a task obviously not
within her power, but she seemed to have a great fondness
for lost causes. I miss her sometimes, and at other junctures,
not at all. Her skirts swished discreetly. She once disguised
herself as a beech tree. Actually, it was a beautifully conceived
Halloween costume. What did it mean that she often talked
about *The Exhaustion of the Masculine*, that she took a course in
Spiritual Warfare, that some nights she seemed to have spared
my life, or that one evening after I'd said something unkind,
she acted confused, pretending not to know what had hurt her?
She liked a lot of ice in her drinks. She loved to propose toasts.
She was a terrible photographer. More than half the people and
animals she took snapshots of ended up decapitated. I gave her
money I didn't even have. It's possible there were days I felt
hollow when she wasn't home. It's possible that I held
that against her. She always seemed to know what time it was
by instinct. She cried extremely easily. She played cello
pretty well. She's still alive, but since we parted, I prefer to
think of her as *late*, as in *tardy* or *delayed*, to believe that someday
when I return home she'll be here, having decorated the house
with white bougainvillea, which she knows I like, to surprise me.

Rash

She made rash decisions and one of them had been to become involved with the dermatologist. A single mother of six-month-old Walter, she had not expected to fall for a pediatric dermatologist who cured Walt's rash, which turned out to be something called diaper dermatitis. As the doctor had promised, the rash vanished after letting the baby go diaper-less for ten days, a messy yet practical solution that delighted her in its simplicity and lack of consequences for small, wriggling Walt.

The dermatologist's name was Rashid, which means "rightly guided." He told her this on their first date, as they left for the movie. He had a nice voice, refined but with a small male burr or purr in it, and a slight British accent.

They'd gone to see the new big-budget space film. It involved the potential exodus of humans from a befouled, increasingly uninhabitable Earth. Against a background of dark blue firmament pricked by zillions of stars, spacecraft in life-or-death situations kept attempting to dock at a space station. Docking sequences were long and slow, backed by rising, triumphal music. These scenes featured a part of the spaceship resembling a length of industrial-sized PVC pipe extending closer and closer to the center of a giant metal daisy, the port on the space station, whose chunky, movable petals were meant to grip and hold the looming cylindrical fixture.

She tried to make herself interested in the movie by telling herself the docking looked sexual. She wondered, Do I Want Rashid to Lock onto Me? She decided if he tried, she would let him. She hoped he hated the movie. It might be difficult to have sex with someone truly enthused about cinematic drivel. When she peeked at Rashid, his eyes seemed fixed on the screen. She didn't know him well enough to tell by looking at his profile whether he was enjoying the movie. Normally she was not a fan of beards, but his was glossy and thick and she wanted to touch it.

Driving back to Rashid's after the movie, she asked if he had a favorite film. "*Rashomon*," he responded. "These priests in ancient Japan are trying to get to the bottom of a murder. The dead victim testifies via a medium. The cinematographer had to lie on his belly to get a lot of the shots. It's raining like crazy in the film. Kind of like now," he observed, switching the wipers to high.

Rashid admitted he'd disliked the space movie, had considered suggesting they leave. Hearing this she felt a quick sizzle up her spine, and shivered. Rashid turned up the heat in the car. Her first sex after childbirth felt rightly guided. Next morning, Rashid brought her breakfast in bed: toast, a glass of milk, coffee, a small bowl of blueberries, and a rasher of bacon. It was still raining. Despite the sadness that eventually ensued on all sides, she fondly remembered that breakfast.

After sex,

       panting and damp, you watch from bed as elder presences assemble. They flicker in and out of visibility in time with your breathing. Sparks dart through your head in quick figure eights. Someone's still chasing someone else through a forest. A tiny dinosaur takes a series of hops, morphs into a bird, gets airborne. In the past, you've been picked up by god and hurled like a fastball against cinderblock walls. But tonight, it's different. You've been pitched onto clean, butter-colored sheets, your body translated into high-minded music. And there's someone beached with you. This is his room. The night sky is black tea, steeping. Jazz standards and the cries of night birds sluice from your pores, their old and new eloquences like flutes heard through fog, suffusing the room.

Conference with the Dead

The things that tethered them to life:
belief in reason, prolonged applause,
nerve cells which fizz as sparklers do,
the pinkening of a lover's ears,
cakes nicely iced and crammed with cream,
the clack of crows, tequila's down-
the-gullet hiss, the gift of having
lips and hips, all of this
is lost to them, while we're still in
the thick of it. No brag, just fact.
So, you may ask: Why did a committee
of the dead demand we living
meet with them? Rage rose off them
in toxic mist. We coughed a lot,
in that bright room at an otherwise dark
primary school we had reserved
for this strange meeting. Maps and leaves
and alphabet charts and children's art
were pinned to walls. Iguanas slept
in their terrarium. Vines curled up
from plastic cups. But just as soon as
we convened, the dead picked fights
among themselves, as though we live ones
weren't there. Like pamphlets scattered
from a plane, their talk at first
made little sense. Two tried and tried
to bite each other. *Whose world is it?*
they gasped at last. *Can't we return
and share the Earth?* We signaled that
this could not be. Their time was up.

They'd had their chance. The world was ours,
and they were dirt. When one of us
would try to speak, they'd shout her down.
So much for substantive discussion.
They aired their grudges at great length:
You killed my sister. You got me pregnant,
then skipped town. You broke our ailing
mother's heart. You harmed my son,
made me ashamed of what I said.
You always ate right off my plate
without permission. They yelled and cursed
till it grew light, and children started
filtering in. We teachers hid,
as little kids filled up the room.
Kids set their heavy backpacks down,
hung up their coats, and stowed bag lunches
in their cubbies. *You angry dead,*
go back to bed, the children sang.
You woke too soon. You need more sleep.
The truth will keep. Your suffering's done.
And one by one the dead slunk out
without a word. We teachers nervously
returned. *How'd you do that?* we asked
the kids. *And what's that song?* The children's
silence seemed a code, a cold,
deep-etched Rosetta stone, an old
decree we could not read. *We need*
a drink of juice, they sang. *We want*
Band-Aids, a girl complained. This sort
of thing was all they'd say. That and,
Grown-ups, don't be afraid. You know
those ghosts could not have stayed.

Furniture

Father always hovered slightly to the side
of any conversation. A shy man, he loved jokes,
especially those starring animals. He had a gap
between his front teeth, and slicked-down black
hair. After his demise, his spirit entered a fake
leather armchair, half of a set of two, tall-backed,
a sort of wing chair that had been his favorite
spot for retreat and contemplation. Mother's
spirit (she'd predeceased him by ten years)
entered the matching black leatherette chair
pretty quickly after that. When no one's home,
I sit in the living room, in one of their laps,
and tell them my troubles and small joys. Father
wants to know if we're at war yet. "With these
fools in the White House," he mutters, "it's just
a matter of time." Mother wants to know how
the Dodgers, her favorite baseball team, are doing,
or if I've seen hummingbird nests this spring.
Father says I should take time off, sit in the sun
with my feet up, have a root beer. "You look
like you could use a little shore leave," he says.
Then a door slams. The kids are home.
Something crashes in the kitchen. One kid yells,
"Oh no!" The other sings, "Bryce is in trouble
again!" to which his brother replies, "YOU just
shut UP!" The dog runs in and begins lightly
biting the hem of my skirt. "Well," Dad says, "nice
talking to you, honey. We'll pick up tomorrow
where we left off," and Mother whispers,
"Quiet, you two, or the children will hear."

Fruit Cocktail in Light Syrup

Rocket-shaped Popsicles that dyed your lips blue
were popular when I was a kid. Our era got labeled
"the space age" in honor of some longed-for,
supersonic, utopian future. Another food of my
youth was candy corn, mostly seen on Halloween.
With its striped, triangular "kernels" made
of sugar, wax, and corn syrup, candy corn
was a nostalgic treat, harking back to a past
when humans grew, rather than manufactured,
food. But what was fruit cocktail's secret
meaning? It glistened as though varnished.
Watery, faint of taste, it contained testicular
grapes, wrinkled and pale. Deflated
maraschino cherries. Fan-shaped pineapple
chunks, and squares of bleached peach
and pear. Fruit cocktail's colorlessness,
its lack of connection to anything living
(like tree, seed, or leaf), seemed sad.
A bowl of soupy fruit funeral. No more
nourishing than a child's finger painting,
masquerading as happy appetizer, fruit
cocktail insisted on pretending everything
was OK. Eating it meant you embraced
tastelessness. It meant you were easily fooled.
It meant you'd pretend semblances,
no matter how pathetic, were real, and that
when things got dicey, you'd spurn the truth.
Eating fruit cocktail meant you might deny

that ghosts whirled throughout the house,
got sucked up the chimney on nights
Dad wadded old newspapers, warned you
away from the hearth, and finally lit a fire.

Wilderness Years

The day came when my thought-broth needed
sweetening, so I snuck out the back door of my life.
No one noticed. Rocks in my pocket in lieu of a rosary,
my first goal was to outdrink every man at the bar. I
didn't get far. The most expressive parts of my face
went numb. An epic swim toward Fortunate Island
seemed in order. Kisses were not as stirring as one
might have liked. Violin music still worked its magic
at night, if the bluish mood lighting was just right.
A long hike to the Charisma Center felt called for. Still
lost in this forest, I crave one bright lamp seen from afar,
and a pill tucked under my tongue to light my way home.

Black Coat

after he falls asleep I'm not ready to lie down
so I make a pilgrimage to the 24-hour
coffee shop at Franklin and Vine and sit at
the counter coat-collar turned up like I'm
an old-time movie detective when in fact
I look like a stubbed-out cigarette tonight
I order Sprite and pie the filling's got way
too much cornstarch I sip soda and fork-
poke gummy blueberry goo take off my coat
and drape it over my lap the old guy two stools
away has about as much hair as a newborn
he's staring at a covered glass cake dish like
it's a UFO the alien pilot inside a big blinding
white slice of coconut cake the man has
deformed ears folded like tacos ears of
a different animal a bat maybe my husband
once tore the screen door off its hinges
heaved a suitcase full of clothes out the window
and it burst so the lawn became a crazy yard sale
he gave me a concussion once shoved me up
against the window of a piñata store as we walked
home from a bar because I said I wanted to leave
he threw a plate of spaghetti and meatballs straight
up into the air tomato sauce dripped from the ceiling
which my son thought was hilarious when he was
three a long time ago I tried to hug my husband
from behind and he grabbed me judo-flipped
me over his shoulder onto the floor but that was
my bad since I startled him I woke up one morning
with his boot print on my cheek there's something

about hearing a man cry that twists the listener's guts
like bus gears grinding people always see my husband's
brilliance gleaming like buried glints of the sweet smart
kid he must have been this coffee shop's unforgiving
light makes me feel like a hologram oh devoted black coat
with button-in lining lying across my lap like a blanket
dear coat you will never see Macau again the place
your label says you were made which after a Google search
on my iPhone I find is in China a former Portuguese colony
famous for gambling so likely you were sewn by slaves
pretty shitty but I can't give up a coat who has been
my protector for so many years this is truly vile pie
behind the counter in the mirror-backed case high
on the wall where Jell-O in parfait glasses and halved
grapefruits are displayed it looks like my neck might be
beginning to bruise guess I'd better pay the bill
and cruise home before it gets light

plays faintly on a neighbor's radio. This makes her think
of a boy she once kind of loved who sang Beatles songs
in his sleep. Just random snatches. Or sometimes a line
from Creedence Clearwater Revival. His face innocent
while sleep-singing. Not that the two of them were as far
from childhood back then as they liked to pretend. The
boy had a nice clear tenor, and a good ear. Night after
night she'd drive straight to his place from the hospital.
She'd sprint up the stairs and let herself into his tiny
apartment, the never-made bed at its center. No matter
how late, he'd be awake, smoking pot, playing records,
noodling on the guitar. Decades and many relationships
later, she gets into bed, plugs earbuds into her head. The
dog at her feet is pawing the bedspread into a big, soft
rosette nest for himself. Another dog curls up on the rug.
She taps a podcast of an astronomy class. Its promise: *to
make sense of the universe and your place within it,* via lectures
with titles like *A Tour of the Cosmos, The Dark Side of Matter,*
and *Catastrophic Collisions.* This last title, she thinks, describes
her past sexual adventures, including with the musically
talented redhead she's remembered. Blessedly, he never
asked questions when her brother got sick. The redhead
has a wife and daughter now, or so she's heard. He runs
a record company that doesn't make records anymore.
Records are retro technology. Her younger, retro-self
thought sex could cure everything. Sex with the redhead
did make her feel less dread-drenched and stricken. Did
sex erase the pervasive sensation that her brain had been
looted from an ancient grave? No. That sticks with her,
though she's sixty, which seems ridiculous. Her past feels

like fiction. Some days she feels ageless. Other days, she's
the ten-year-old boy who always fidgeted within her, or
the girl to whom trees and insects still send coded messages.
Other animals abide in her too, plus gamma ray bursts and
distant eclipses. *Yeah, yeah,* thinks the dog on the floor, sleepily.
She contains all that. So do we. Dusted with bits of Pluto and Mars,
we're big bang afterglow. We gleam with the brilliance of stars.

Her Last Companion

In her best-known work, the English title of which is
My Hundred Beloveds, he is the thinly disguised final
entry. She viewed herself as fearfully unstable. He
had wanted to protect her. The aquarium provided
the site of their first meeting. In the cool blue light
of the eel tank, while a child nearby fussed in its pram
and shook a rattle at them ("like some kind of shaman,"
he later observed in his diary) they shared their first
kiss. During that visit they took in the kelp forest,
the sea otter pond, red octopi and sheer jellyfish
wafting like dropped handkerchiefs in slow motion.
What was it she reminded him of? Try as he might,
he could never quite catch hold of that. "How could
this happen to me?" she marveled in letters to friends,
adding "his caring for me as he does overwhelms me."
"I am more afraid of myself than I am of you," she
wrote to him in June. In July, "I sometimes feel
that no one has or ever can share anything."
A stringent listener, he praised her small hands.
We have evidence they suffered when apart. In
a small album of photographs, electricity developing
between them is visible as a kind of halo, a faint
glow encompassing them both, merging where they
stand most closely together, though in fact they never
touch in the photographs that survive. His eyes look
wet and attentive in most of the photos. She often
wears one of the big-brimmed hats women favored
at the time. He looks most handsome when bearded.
He is never seen smoking in any of the photos, though
she usually has a cigarette between her lips. Dogs

are often present, frequently spaniels we know
were his. Two pages in his diary are devoted
to cataloging her laughs. "It is startling," he wrote,
"when this delicate creature opens her mouth and emits
a brash, crashing laugh that sounds like metal trash cans
rolling down the street." He kept some of her last
writings till they were confiscated by the Gestapo.
Her intense *yes*, his thin, haggard face: Are these clichés?
Why do I feel tethered to them? Aren't we, as we'd always
comfortably assumed, in speaking a different language,
in another country and era, safe from their fate?
Some say he wrote what's carved on her headstone.
Others insist they collaborated:

    Whatever her griefs, she knew love.

A Monument of Unwashed Dishes

has once again risen in the sink
an archaeological record
of what everyone's eaten this week
so she grabs a scrub pad
twists on the hot water
and leans into the steam

wiping condensation from the window
she can see the ancient widower down the street
plundering neighbors' recycling bins
recently bereaved, the widower wears
his dead wife's sunhat
mashed onto his too-large head
he is tall and scarecrow-like
his clothes look scavenged from the trash
and in the wrecked little hat
with cloth flower pinned to its brim
he seems a ragged tree
impersonating a human
while above him a huge eucalyptus
rustles with squirrels

she clatters spoons into the drying rack
and wonders why her secrets
have lately gained the power of myth
like what happened long ago in a tent
on an island in a lake
filled with sunfish and water snakes
the rusty but functional canoe
overturned on the beach

oars stashed underneath
her bathing suit had a flounced skirt
that's how young she was
a fondle and a squirt and it was over

it's almost not worth scrambling eggs
if they're going to stick to the pan so bad
is it too early for a glass of booze?
she thinks a quick spritz of endorphins
would hit the spot right now

after the initial vodka sip
she believes she could live a different kind of life entirely
perhaps in a tent? could she taste the happiness of saints
in their dark, unwashed garments
living only for herself, god as her alibi?
a saint's joy dry and crumbly
as a handful of stale cake?

children toss a Frisbee across a parched lawn
as streetlights waver on
a girl and dog play under a picnic table
while the mother reads her Sunday paper on the stoop
by porchlight one sister walks outside
holding a spatula and says, "how can anyone
take you seriously with that frosted blue eyeshadow?"
and they laugh

she wipes coffee grounds off the counter
with a towel that's had its personality bleached away
the sun plummets in runny pastels
who knew shame was such a large part of growing older
as though through lack of vigilance you'd slid into ruin

as though drunk in front of everyone you'd fallen
down a flight of stairs

these endless ill-fitting versions of womanhood . . .
should she envision herself as something else?
a flower full of fluorescing nectar?
though aren't those mostly deathtraps for insects?
the green orb of the orange tree
studded with tiny white blossoms
might be nice to be
or maybe a fleet, arboreal creature
who can smell the age and relative health
of each leaf before eating it

a feminine epic lives in her under wraps
like a field of sheet-draped statues
fugitive, incognito
and when some of her ancestors
that chorus of ghost-women finally take her hand
and smooth her hair, they smile in sympathy as
the last of her mother's wineglasses cracks
against the scoured pit of the sink
as the cypress tree sways perilously
when an owl alights on its pinnacle

she takes potatoes from the bin and lights the oven
her guts grumble reminding her
of the sloshing bag of viscera she is

when you love someone is it your duty to tell them?
shouldn't you keep those revelations to yourself?
so far, her strategy has been to construct a hive of silence

to tuck honey away where no one will find it
in residual moments of the day
as the last flaming swipes of orange
abandon the sky to gray

Update

Your dresses huddle in their closet.
No histrionics, no tears. They're undaunted,
unhaunted, since you disappeared.
Torture by laundry and mothball
is all I can offer them. Tomorrow, it's Christmas.
And despite the holiday, about which I'm
listless, there's endless wrestling on TV.
Is that weird programming your nudge
to me: toughen up and roll with the punches?
Here on Earth, another rough era is birthed.
Sea monsters burst from the surf, through
waves of what we've mistaken for civilization.
Any advice from the heights where you're exiled?
Some flutter of succor to dial back the angst
to a dull roar? Though you are no more,
the onions you planted, shoved underground
too, send shoots into this persistent rain,
like little green racks of antlers. Your
azalea's ablaze with reds, magentas,
and noisy finches. The sweetgum tree lost her leaves,
then grew six inches. I'll slip on my coat and hike
to the river, pray I see your image, fringed
by whitewater, in it. If I do, can you gift
me with some savagery-management tips, or a
comforting sign, surreptitiously, via the mist?

{several extant fragments from the *Index of Women*}

and she saved his baby teeth
in a tiny box
that once held a ring.
Teeth like chips of china
flecked with dried blood.

she made careful note of:
—everyone's favorite foods
—what it pleased them to be complimented on
—their preferred places to sit

She was the only archaeologist on the team
small enough to crawl into the cave
to see the toppling white piles
of ancient skulls and bones
and looming cave paintings.

Hers was a different species of beauty.

C-Section and Bad Hair Day are names
she and her bandmates
are considering.

she knows how to cook bruised vegetables
so they taste pretty good
she is equally at home reading
the Dead Sea Scrolls or Vogue,
or making critical acquisitions on her cell.
The first thing she does when she gets home
is wriggle out of her control-top pantyhose

On her days off she's the happiest drunk at the bar,
and when she slips off her jacket
during her third beer, we scrutinize her tattoos.
She claims they date from her time in exile,
when she had left her mother's house,
wandered forty days and nights,
and ended up here.

Woman with Her Throat Slit

Hello,

   Please confirm if you are still alive, because two gentle men worked into my office this morning to claim your Contract funds in our custody. I got your email from one of the files of those who have not been paid for the Contract you or your Parents did. If you are still alive please confirm with your full contact details ASAP for you to receive your payment.

—Derek Langtree

Dear Mr. Langtree,
Your email was uncannily timely. Yes, I'm alive,
thanks for asking, if a bit stricken. Alive, though I've
lost that sweet taste in my mouth of . . . what? That tang
of everlastingness in the transitory, like a note of rust
in gulped water? My breasts feel like hand grenades
about to explode, Mr. Langtree. A heaviness in my
gut suggests someone cut me open as I slept,
and filled my body's pockets with rocks. The sight
of my face is a disquieting surprise, like stepping
on a snake. Mr. Langtree, which I'm aware
isn't your real name, I'm in mourning. Between
the teeth of a disconcerting grief. Wouldn't you say
the brain's crenulations rival the topography
of the Himalayas? Don't you agree that while
the feet seem meek, they harbor darker knowledge
than the easy-to-please hands? By praising parts
of the body I'm hoping to call them home, or
at least to locate myself. One grows tired of reciprocity,
of nodding, of fixing one's hair. One snarls in one's
sleep. The body leaks secrets.

Someone I loved decades ago, with the full force
of what I was then, died, a suicide, in his parked car.
This news appeared in a paper to which I subscribe
and which I read during morning coffee. I haven't
spoken to him in thirty years, though I probably
dreamed of him weekly during that time. Back
in our day I craved praise, declarations. We both
did things of which we were later ashamed. He came
to see me as a trap and was thus right to flee. Still.
I could not swallow my low-acid coffee or anything
else today after reading his obituary, squinting at
its grainy picture. Someone, I felt, not for the first
time in my life, had drawn a knife lightly across my
neck. Then came your fake email.

As for the payment you mention, please keep it,
Mr. Langtree. Easy for me to be free with
fictitious money. You're an internet swindler.
How do you feel about that? I imagine you have
your reasons. I don't want to be awake any
longer this evening, reduced to writing a thief
who doesn't have the guts to case neighborhoods
and jimmy windows and instead siphons cash
from the gullible across a faceless international
netscape. Mr. Langtree, did you know, growing
old is violent, like being kidnapped, like waking up
to find your throat slit while you're still alive and
able to burble words? And getting elderly has not
quieted the feral girl who's crouched inside me
for as long as I can recall. To most people I've
become about as interesting as a papercut.
But I digress.

I think I'll take a sleeping pill to stanch
consciousness for a while. So much can spill
out of a woman whose throat has been slit.
Gasps, demands, viola solos. I promised my
doctor not to talk like this anymore. But I can
speak to you any way I like, can't I, Mr. Langtree?
I promised the doc to be more vulnerable and honest,
though I've lost the knack for honesty if ever I had it.
Perhaps you have similar feelings? I promised the doc
to stop telling that sordid, self-congratulatory
fairy tale written on my underwear, to quit insisting
on the validity of that narrational panty-stain the shape
of an island of which I crowned myself queen. I
promised her to abandon my unhealthy former self
and forge a new one, complete with a fresh set of legends
about my backstory. I just need someone to hand me
my Styrofoam sword and cardboard shield, to drape
my bath towel cloak gently about my shoulders.
The thing about a woman with her throat slit is how
much more can pour out of her now. We females
being just heaps of seeping orifices with the power
to drown, one more perforation just cranks up
the music. Perhaps you feel I'm drowning you now,
if you've persisted in reading this. I hope so. Even
when she's lying on the floor, trying to sleep,
her arms budding into Venus flytraps and her legs
elongating into cutlery, you can't shut up a woman with
her throat cut. Do you think, Mr. Langtree, that
either of us will ever regain that sweet taste in our
mouths? Do you regret losing it too? If I prayed I
would pray not to dream about you.

Woman Looking at a Drop of Seawater Under the Microscope

Who knew this little bit of spillage
contained multitudes of what we all

boil down to? Microorganisms
swim a surface the wet silver

of Poseidon's eyes. Spiralized lines,
pulsing globules, tiny sacs filled with aspic.

Obscenely, you can see right through
them, sometimes down to their nuclei.

They come in lovely colors.
Is this natural or has the scientist

who slid their slide under the microscope
stained them orange, ocher, and blue

for better viewing? Their outlines
waver like hand-drawn cartoons.

They resemble party favors,
tiny offspring of a bubble cluster

and the plankton alphabet.
Why, then, have I been so afraid

of what I am made of breaking down
into constituent parts, of one day

rejoining this infinitesimal assembly,
of becoming an orgy of particles

too (beautiful and) numerous to count?

Happy Hour

Quid datur a divis felici optatius hora?
What is there given by the gods more desirable than a happy hour?

—Catullus

Sacred days and scathing days.
Blown off course
by grieving a dead friend
so keenly it pangs the roots
of the teeth. Noon.
A day moon floats,
gray eminence
with a bad complexion,
hung like a piñata
above this hummingbird
who feints and whirs
at trumpet flowers.
One wants to touch
the bird like a page
of braille, read its
speedy heartbeats,
but can one ever be
that gentle? Everything
seems out of reach.
One blast of air from
the glassblower's lungs
hovers inside the vase
he's shaping. How unchastely
grateful, how shaken by
life-thirst and yearning
this world has made me.

Jellyfish Brains

Seems like we'd just started to make tools,
to bury our dead so predators couldn't eat them.
Didn't we domesticate animals just yesterday?
Wasn't it only a month or so ago we first hollowed
out grindstones? Didn't we just master pottery?
It all happened so fast. How long since we first
learned to herd camels, since we figured out how
deliciously wind fills the bellies of sails? Didn't we
start carving figurines only recently, the ones
we hang round our necks, little pocket gods to rub
when we're scared? Feels like we raced straight
from clay tablets to parchment to paperbacks
in a day. Invented medicines along the way.
First danced to bring rain yesterday. Minted
coins only lately, money playing no small role
in our downfall. I read that a jellyfish's brains whirl
in her skirts, that plants are really slow, rooted
animals, that elephants dig their own wells. Who
begat this miraculous world, shaped from nothing
but sunlight and mud? Who let loose that universal
music, more lovely than anything made by the hand
of man, that sometimes arrives out of silence?

Giraffes

acting as if nothing terrible has happened
is a failed strategy you yell and this docility
has ruined and crushed us and afraid as I am
I cannot hold your vehemence against you
at this political moment as I watch you dig
your fingers into the rubble you're sitting on
and you say maybe it's impossible to believe
in politeness or civilization anymore and you say
complacency has bitten us with rabid hyena teeth
for being blind to the suffering of those we thought
were not like us at all and you say silence
and indifference have brought us this dead end
and you are fresh out of cheeks to turn
so from this day forward no more hiding in the attic
no more sheltering in place in the balcony or orchestra
as oboes tune up no more sublimating your rape
because the rapist was famous no more huddling
on the patio for comet-watching parties at 2 a.m.
marveling as stars shoot across the hallowed blackness
now that the rain has turned to drops of molten glass
alas no more celebrating the chutzpah of elderly
skydivers only gallows humor now and vain attempts
to comfort the young whose inheritance we have
squandered the young who you insist are better
at comforting us with the sincerity of their terror
only last-ditch activism you say will be coin of the realm
only tremulous toasts with booze you won't save
for special occasions anymore only whispered salutes
to survival since power-drunk clowns have taken over
the circus and loosed the lions exacting revenge

for being laughed at and that ancient mound
in the backyard you've thrown yourself down on
was once a thriving household archaeologists say
they learned this by analyzing their trash and these
ancestors painted pottery and kept cows and
composed songs and before that the dirt mound
you've repurposed as a weeping couch was just
a sneeze of rock vapor way out in space you're going
to miss this Earth, you say, how the sky turns smoky red
on some summer nights good ol' planet Earth home
of the meatball omelet home of media spin of whatever
bigoted muck humans dream up home of maidenhair
ferns dripping after a downpour home of snow and of
every kind of body and feeler and tentacle every manner
of sex and home of stately giraffes tame enough to eat
from your hand though that involves such a stretch
for them it folds them in half how do these treelike
creatures swoop their heads down so gracefully
bowing so low and in a weird voice I ask if you still
love me or can even think about that now and you
stare for a second and say in this bleak upheaval
that was never up for grabs, so I'd like to reveal that
I went straight from our backyard to the zoo and
freed the giraffes and all the wronged animals and
conferred with them about government overthrow
but I haven't done anything that revolutionary, yet

ACKNOWLEDGMENTS

Huge thanks to the Guggenheim Foundation and the Foundation for Contemporary Arts for their invaluable support of the writing of this book. Thank you to Penguin Random House.

The following people have my gratitude:
The late Tom Clark, Bernard Cooper, Dennis Cooper, Jim Gunderson, Steve Gunderson, Dorna Khazeni, Michelle Latiolais, David Lehman, Dinah Lenney, Jeffrey McDaniel, Eileen Myles, Michael Ryan, Paul Slovak, Alexis Smith, Louise Steinman, Gail Swanlund, David Trinidad, Irina Tsoy, Jane Weinstock, and Matthew Zapruder.

Poems in this book previously appeared in the following publications (thank you!), sometimes in slightly different forms:

Academy of American Poets Poem-a-Day: "To a Head of Lettuce," "Poof," and "Fruit Cocktail in Light Syrup."
Brief Encounters, an anthology edited by Dinah Lenney and Judith Kitchen: "Viennese Pathology Museum."
Columbia Poetry Review: "Happy Hour," "'All You Need Is Love,'" "My Ego," and "Virginity."
Court Green: "Night Life," "Anthem," and "Buried Song."
F Magazine: "After sex."
Fifth Wednesday Journal: "Dead Butterfly."
4ink7: "Translation" and "How Happy I Was When Mother Bought Me Those Three Dresses."

Gianthology: "Conference with the Dead" and "Furniture."

Literary Matters: "Tooth Fairy Sonnet" and "Woman with Her Throat Slit."

Los Angeles Review of Books: "Rash" and "Giraffes."

Lungfull! Magazine: "Gender Is Fluid" and "Crystal Blue Persuasion."

Memorious: "A Monument of Unwashed Dishes."

Ploughshares: "Glimpse," "Update," and "My Late Wife."

The poem "Letters from a Lost Doll" appeared in an exhibition catalog for the *Not I* show, published by the Los Angeles County Museum of Art. The show was curated by José Luis Blondet.

NOTES

PAGE 3 "{from an Introduction to some fragments of the *Index of Women*}" contains phrases, quotations, and/or bent quotations from the following texts: Hesiod's *Catalogue of Women*; the Girl Scout pledge as it read in the 1970s; *Combat Integration Handbook*, 2016; Joseph Campbell's *The Hero with a Thousand Faces*; various reference sources on the Greek goddess Hecate; and an article titled "Li Qingzhao, poet, 'the most talented woman in history,'" which can be found here: https://supchina .com/2020/04/06/li-qingzhao-poet-the-most-talented-woman-in-history/. The phrase "ghosts before breakfast," which ends the poem, is the English title of a short German Dada film by Hans Richter, circa 1928.

PAGE 10 "Ode to Birth Control" contains two references to Margaret Sanger (1879–1966). Sanger was a nurse who coined the term "birth control." She was a social activist, writer, early feminist, and campaigner for women's reproductive rights. During the editing of this book, Penguin copy editor Jean Hartig called to my attention news stories on Margaret Sanger's connection to eugenics and racism. I am grateful to her for making me aware of this and the resulting serious controversies surrounding Sanger's legacy, which have led me to reconsider my feelings about her. More information on this topic is available here: www.nytimes .com/2020/07/21/nyregion/planned-parenthood-margaret-sanger- eugenics.html. The phrase "until men and women are absolved from the fear of becoming parents, except when they themselves desire it" is a quote from a pamphlet published in 1830 by Robert Dale Owen called *Moral Physiology, or, A Brief and Plain Treatise on the Population Question.*

PAGE 16 "An Aging Opera Singer Speaks at Her First AA Meeting" mentions Renée Fleming, the extraordinary opera singer who was born on Valentine's Day, 1959, and Sei Shōnagon (circa 966–1025), author of a marvelous and singular work that has come down to us in English as *The Pillow Book of Sei Shōnagon*.

PAGE 23 "Crystal Blue Persuasion" mentions Charon, who in ancient Greek mythology was tasked with ferrying the souls of the dead across two rivers to the underworld. The title of the poem is the title of a 1969 song by Tommy James and the Shondells. The line in the poem "strive diligently / work consciously" is one of several translations of what some believe were the last words of the Buddha.

PAGE 33 "Letters from a Lost Doll" contains several quotes and/or bent quotations from Isabelle Eberhardt's book *The Oblivion Seekers*, Paul Bowles translation.

PAGE 41 "Earth, Temple, Gods" is inspired by a body of work by visual artist James Welling entitled *Archaeology*.

PAGE 42 "Translation" is for Dorna Khazeni.

PAGE 45 "The Semmelweis Opera": Ignaz Semmelweis (1818–1865) was a Hungarian doctor and scientific researcher. There is a medical museum named after him in Budapest. He is revered today for advocating handwashing as a means of infection control, but was ridiculed during his lifetime for his ideas about antisepsis, as the poem describes.

PAGE 49 "Horizontal Women" takes its title from an artwork by John Baldessari.

PAGE 64 "All You Need Is Love" is the title of a 1967 song by the Beatles.

PAGE 66 In "Her Last Companion" there are several lines from a letter Virginia Woolf wrote to Leonard Woolf on May 1, 1912, that have been slightly altered into lines in the poem.

PAGE 75 The title "Woman with Her Throat Slit" is a slight corruption of the title of a sculpture by Alberto Giacometti, usually translated into English as *Woman with Her Throat Cut*, dating from the early 1930s.

Phrases from *The I Ching, or Book of Changes*, Richard Wilhelm translation, appear in several poems in this book.

AMY GERSTLER'S thirteen books of poems include *Scattered at Sea* (Penguin, 2015), which was longlisted for the National Book Award, shortlisted for the Kingsley Tufts Poetry Award, and a finalist for the PEN America Literary Award. Her book *Dearest Creature* (Penguin, 2009) was named a *New York Times* Notable Book, and was shortlisted for the Los Angeles Times Book Prize in Poetry. Her previous twelve books include *Ghost Girl, Medicine, Crown of Weeds, Nerve Storm,* and *Bitter Angel,* which won a National Book Critics Circle Award. She received a Guggenheim Fellowship in 2018. In 2019 she received a C.D. Wright Award from the Foundation for Contemporary Arts. She was the 2010 guest editor of the yearly anthology *The Best American Poetry.* Her work has appeared in a variety of magazines and anthologies, including *The New Yorker, The Paris Review, The American Poetry Review, Poetry,* several volumes of *The Best American Poetry,* and *Postmodern American Poetry: A Norton Anthology.* She has written art criticism and exhibition catalog essays for the Whitney Museum of American Art, the Museum of Contemporary Art Los Angeles, *Artforum* magazine, and other publications. She is currently working on a musical play with composer/actor Steve Gunderson and on a children's book.

PENGUIN POETS

PATRICIA LOCKWOOD
*Motherland Fatherland
    Homelandsexuals*

WILLIAM LOGAN
Macbeth in Venice
Madame X
Rift of Light
Strange Flesh
The Whispering Gallery

J. MICHAEL MARTINEZ
Museum of the Americas

ADRIAN MATEJKA
The Big Smoke
Map to the Stars
Mixology

MICHAEL MCCLURE
*Huge Dreams: San Francisco
    and Beat Poems*

ROSE MCLARNEY
Forage
Its Day Being Gone

DAVID MELTZER
*David's Copy: The Selected
    Poems of David Meltzer*

ROBERT MORGAN
Dark Energy
Terroir

CAROL MUSKE-DUKES
Blue Rose
*An Octave Above Thunder:
    New and Selected Poems*
Red Trousseau
Twin Cities

ALICE NOTLEY
Certain Magical Acts
Culture of One
The Descent of Alette
Disobedience
For the Ride
In the Pines
Mysteries of Small Houses

WILLIE PERDOMO
The Crazy Bunch
*The Essential Hits of Shorty
    Bon Bon*

DANIEL POPPICK
Fear of Description

LIA PURPURA
*It Shouldn't Have Been
    Beautiful*

LAWRENCE RAAB
The History of Forgetting
*Visible Signs: New and
    Selected Poems*

BARBARA RAS
The Last Skin
One Hidden Stuff

MICHAEL ROBBINS
Alien vs. Predator
The Second Sex

PATTIANN ROGERS
Generations
Holy Heathen Rhapsody
Quickening Fields
Wayfare

SAM SAX
Madness

ROBYN SCHIFF
A Woman of Property

WILLIAM STOBB
Absentia
Nervous Systems

TRYFON TOLIDES
*An Almost Pure Empty
    Walking*

VINCENT TORO
Tertulia

SARAH VAP
Viability

ANNE WALDMAN
Gossamurmur
Kill or Cure
Manatee/Humanity
Trickster Feminism

JAMES WELCH
Riding the Earthboy 40

PHILIP WHALEN
Overtime: Selected Poems

ROBERT WRIGLEY
*Anatomy of Melancholy and
    Other Poems*
Beautiful Country
Box
*Earthly Meditations: New and
    Selected Poems*
Lives of the Animals
Reign of Snakes

MARK YAKICH
*The Importance of Peeling
    Potatoes in Ukraine*
Spiritual Exercises
*Unrelated Individuals
    Forming a Group Waiting
    to Cross*